mediocre maladaptive melodrama

brianne wojtowicz christensen

Presentation by *BookLeaf Publishing*

Web: www.bookleafpub.com

E-mail: info@bookleafpub.com

ISBN: 9789363309883

First edition 2024

for the liliths, judiths, & hagars of the world,
and for the God who sees...

ACKNOWLEDGEMENT

thank you to Jesus, my parents, every teacher or professor who has inspired me, the council of nicaea, anne carson for doing the Lord's work and translating sappho's fragments, peter green for the excellent and very british translation of catullus' corpus, twenty one pilots, flannery o'connor (for obvious reasons), and iced oat milk lattes.

PREFACE

reading back the poems i wrote for this book, they're pretty emotional. it suits me well, as i have always been a very emotional person. i've always been sensitive and theatrical with a remarkably low pain tolerance. this quality of mine along with a few other elements of my personality have made it increasingly challenging to get through this life. and i've often felt alone and alienated. my hope for this book is that someone just like me will read these poems and know that they are not the only person in the world to experience the desolation and destruction of a sick mind. the authors and lyricists who have provided me with weapons to fight off the feeling of isolation have been my safe port in all of my cerebral storms and my life would finally have purpose to it if i could do that for someone else. my intention in publishing this small collection of mediocre musings is this: there are no unique experiences, but you will never understand that unless someone with your experience puts it into the most powerful form of art, words. dear reader, you are not alone.

sinner that i am

my Lord, my God, my Savior
i have denied You 300 times.
i am peter,
i am thomas,
i am judas.
i throw my 30 silver coins at the mirror with
every ounce of strength in my body,
shattering the glass tear-stained face
staring back at me.
her countenance has fallen,
i have broken her with my own two hands.

my roman knuckles swell,
the bruised soreness recalls
my fist's grip around the hammer
that pounded the nails into the Man of Sorrows'
holy hands,
which have healed me
70 x 7 times.

the cross is hoisted.
i drop the hammer.
with agonized humiliation
and eyes refusing to ascend,
i trod toward the splintered wood,

with trembling bones.
my knees collide with golgotha's soil.

i think about who You are,
i am terrified of what i have become.
i beg the suffering servant
lamentable and slain,
for mercy.

surrender

the thing
the feeling
it's like an ache
it begins in my stomach
a seed planted deep in my being
watered by the warmth of the crimson rushing
through my veins
running late as always.
it grows and grows with every expansion of my
lungs
it's taking over.
an invisible tidal wave crashing over my bones,
threatening to snap with the urgency of a dying
atheist,
but never following through on its promises.
inside of me is a bottomless well of water colder
than the atlantic.
i'm being pulled into it.
i think i've forgotten how to write poetry.

depart from me

so you think God will have mercy on you?
you think you could go to heaven?
after everything you've done,
everywhere you've been,
the crimson blood that stains your hands and
wrists,
the scars on His temple.

you had a halo,
gently glowing like the flame of a candle.
but it burned out a long,
long,
long time ago.

"I REBUKE THE SPIRIT OF REGRET!"
you spit as the shattered mirror glares back at
you.
there's venom on your lips
and tears spill over your cheeks and drip
down your face.
it is too late.
you know where you're going.

tomorrow,
if you don't wake up,

you'll find yourself in flames under the earth.
if not,
you'll be drowsy under the covers.
the clock moves on without you.
time is not your friend.
it's time to get up and get ready for work.

sappho's curse

i mean i knew i was demented,
but this is ridiculous.
i hope my thoughts are meaningless,
just a
harmless
little
tiny
itty
bitty

crush.

no it's massive.

i can't listen to love songs
because i've started seeing her face in the
swelling chords.
she's in my dreams.
it's so mean.
i just want her to talk to me.

i'm breaking my back for her to notice.
can you hear the snaps of my bones
as i reach and stretch for meaning

where there is only my pathetic little heart
beating?
like an old vinyl record
that no one has any interest in hearing.
broken and busted,
i can't ever trust it.
because it loves all the wrong things,
like girls.

i hope she never knows,
the only upward spiral i've ever seen in my life
is the corners of my mouth when she starts
talking.
i'm keeping high walls around myself,
high enough that,
should i climb down,
i'll kill myself from the vastness of the drop to
the ground.
i'll fall harder than icarus,
harder than lucifer,
a sky worshipper who will die on the ground.

she ruined my life.
when i saw her eyes
for the third or fourth time,
and i realized,
horrified,
but not surprised,
of course it would be a girl that i like.

because my
bloody,
beaten,
bruised,
dysfunctional heart
loves all the wrong things,
like girls.

and i'll die and go to hell
before anyone knows
why i laugh at all those stupid unfunny jokes.

corset

wrap your arms around my waist
make me feel safe.
dig your nails into my skin,
make my jeans fit,
make me thin.

sit up straight,
won't arch my back.
won't bend over,
lest a rib cracks.

i will live in you like the Holy Spirit,
i'll treasure you like a critical vein.
though i am weak and in pain.
'til you're torn and your edges are frayed,
wrap your arms around my waist.

so i can play pretend.
so i won't be afraid.
so i won't be ashamed.
so i will be an hourglass.
so i will be an angel.

be gentle.

eschatology

there are so many candles in this church.
it's just asking to be burnt to the ground.
then you'll find me underneath the smithereens
when Heaven's tears come raining down.
i'll climb the raindrops like a stairway to home.
the purest thing i've ever known.
the sorrows in our lady's eyes
tend to hide from us in plain sight.
Gethsemane won't fall too far out of mind.
may Heaven's tears put out the fire,
silence the flames that i've inspired.
the phone booth trembles at the sound it makes
on Judgement Day.
and i can only hope it's saint peter calling,
because i am not stalling…
nor have i ever.

sky worshipper

sky worshipper,
you've fallen down so far.
sky worshipper,
you hit the road awfully hard.

the sun is burning holes in your scars.
she said you fall away but never stray too far.
her golden rays carry you home.
sky worshipper,
you are not your own.

the clouds tower over you,
the sky lives in your eyes.
red and orange,
black and blue,
the mourning's arrival is always a surprise.

golden sun and crystal moon,
why do the seasons turn so soon?
do you love me like i love you?
warmth always leaves with the afternoon.

but you are so beautiful.

sky worshipper,
welcome home.

great minds think alike

we are broken from the start.
you have my heart.
i know what it means to fall apart.
and i know your heart.
i'll stop them before they tear it apart.

the thorn remains tangled in your side
as mobs of townsfolk twist their knives.
hidden deep within the walls of your skull
lays a mine of gold,
they will never see through.

i myself am a thesis statement with a question
mark.
there is no one-word answer in the dictionary
that could pick my semantics apart.
my hands are my own,
they do not belong to the dictionary.
there is a person beyond the category.

behind my eyes and above the hands wrapped
around my throat,
is a masterpiece that you will never know.
deranged as i am,
you must understand:

that i am my only home.
my psyche is not always my friend,
but it's all i truly know.
and i treasure it close.

O ye of so little faith

my name is brianne,
but call me thomas.
if i'm being honest,
i don't believe in anything
or anyone who speaks.

i am a field of long wavy grass,
breaking my back
by the face of a gentle breeze.
the only thing that i believe is that i don't believe
in anything.
i freeze.
i breathe.
with staggered breaths and an ache in my chest.
and certainly,
someone's god will punish me.
because i cannot seem to believe in anything.

my religion is doubt.
i was raised in a foreign homeland house.
falling away
all on my own.
i don't know right now.
maybe egypt has been the promised land all
along.

the nile a river of honey
bearing blessings
of dirty hands and bloody money.
but i don't know.
it's doubtful, i suppose.

i am a plane that was built with faulty parts

you'll run away.
you're just like me.
the stars aligned for a time,
but gone is the night.
the sun is risen
and she demands a sacrifice.
so i'll see you some other time.
and maybe you'll see me too and say hi.

i'm missing so much,
hiding away in the dark attic of my mind.
in a nightmare.
i can't do anything right.
i think i will die,
i mean it this time.

then comes daylight,
shattered glass and tattered metal.
i hit the brake when i should've hit the pedal.
and now i'm learning to fly,
projectile.
like a brick through a window,
like a body through a windshield.

i am covered in blood,
covered in mud.
covered in my sins.
i'm almost done.

ill fated,
dreams faded.
counting down the days.
do you hear that ticking?
is it the bomb under your bed?
is it the grandfather clock inside of my head?
not too long and i think i'll be dead.

i'm losing my mind again.
someone please find me.

please.

set your affection on things above

what if there's a Higher Power?
what if i could be with Him?
a Beneficent God,
Whose love could wash
the scars from my skin.
and if such a Spirit were to exist,
how couldn't i leave to be with Him?
how could i choose a broken earth,
an empty tank devoid of worth,
over the skies?
why should i lift my eyes
to where i want to be,
when i could close them tight
and find a route to flee?
i'm afraid my faith has gotten lost in my anxiety.
this desert sand is meaningless to me
until i see it building pyramids in the bottom half
of the hourglass.

sharp things

if i start to count my scars,
one, two three, four…
i will start seeing stars,
because i still want more.
i can't say why
i admire what they look like.
no one else gets to see
no one else but me.

mom says they're like train tracks,
dusty old faded white.
underneath my skin.
from years ago
when i stopped taking my medicine.
up & down.
inside & out.
red like wine.
and zig zags from the times
i ran out of room,
but not out of night.
i'm an artist.
i work on my masterpiece
until i've had enough for now and i fall asleep.
in the mourning i wake
and curse the risen sun.

because it's another day.

sleeves
i need sleeves as long as this life feels.
if i give them a reason to think that the pills
aren't working,
they will know i'm a liar.
i say i am fine.
i will be fine.

what good is it to take me to the hospital one
more time?
i will take more pills as prescribed
i will continue to lie
i'll leave with a mind still terminally ill
and you'll get another emergency room bill.
and it's my life to end, anyway.
you of all people shouldn't want me to stay.
and why can i never write anything without
getting suicidal about it.

risen

empty parking lots,
vacant skies.
i can feel you watch
with your starless eyes.
too broken and too drunk to realize
that the sun rises in the mourning,
but only when you're alive to see it.

yes, the sun will rise
and melt away the ice.
she'll kiss the scars on your skin until they fade
away.
tomorrow she'll shine twice as bright
just so you can see the light
and know,
everything will be alright.
but only if you stay the night.

the world feels deserted,
and you think you're alone.
in the middle of nowhere.
a house but no home.
the sky,
once grey,
is monotone black with night.

and i can see that you're going down without a
fight.

you say you're too far gone,
but you're right in front of me.
you say you've got no one,
but i'm right in front of you.
the darkness is swallowing you whole,
feels like your body has left your soul.
you're starting to turn the door knob,
so i cry out one last time:

stay the night.
a couple hours from now,
the window will be brighter than the last time
you looked.
you will see the pink orange paint that disrupts
the black ink on the page.
the mountains are lined with gold.
with time,
the dark will fade and you will realize
you have won your fight.
and the sun will be
risen.

sleepy days

i bought a bottle of melatonin,
and swallowed the whole thing yesterday.
i washed each pill down with black coffee.
sleep is the only thing that makes life worth
living.

the doctor upped the dosage on one or a few of
my meds.
i'm explosive.
i need chemicals to keep my vision from going
red.
the bottles are kept in a safe
with the key far away
from me.
sometimes i can't control my impulsivity.
i don't know how i'm still alive.
by now i should've died.
i have lived far too much life.
my faces have aged visibly.
never thought in my worst nightmares i'd grow
up to be a dyke.
mortality is on my mind.
i'm still trying to put myself together,
although i've gotten better.

dehydrated

aging blood stains
like splatters of paint
fading away
sinking into a white pillowcase
not too long before it's covered in stains
mascara and tears
expired dreams and growing pains.

a rubber tourniquet is wrapped tightly around
my arm
so tight my fingertips are tinted blue
they are numb like the rest of me.
my bones are growing feeble.
sitting in another cold room,
waiting for another needle.
i'm wide awake
while the nurse concentrates,
searching for a vein.
she finds it and sinks the needle in.
i try not to think about the spear inside my skin.
i try to breathe away the pain.
i hear her say something about me not eating or
drinking enough today.
and she can't get the syringe full enough.

i'm fine.

j'ai créé un monde

in my mind,
j'ai créé un monde.
a screaming silent film with lighters and
cigarettes,
tragedy and dismal epithets.
but really and truly,
i'm just lost in my head.
staring into an endless outer space,
dreaming of a made-up thriller novel place.
romance and calamity,
shades of blue in the minor key.
ghastly and grim,
macabre and red lipstick,
ironically melancholic harlequin.

every character is morally grey,
good-natured smiles are totally faked,
their knees are bruised and scraped,
yet they still kneel and pray,
every single night,
just in case.
i'd ask them if they're okay,
but i already know,
ho creato questo mondo.
i'm the writer,

saturated in blue and ever inspired.
my hands are on fire but my eyes are tired.

what if i had a lighter,
a cigarette,
and some elegant smoke?
it would look so delicate.
so cinematic, isn't it?
but it lingers in my throat,
and pollutes my lungs.
i start to choke,
and as my eyes tear up,
the thought occurs,
the realm of my mindless daydream prose,
it's not quite the way i hoped.
in spite of the lingering phantom smoke,
the corners of my lips curl upward in pride.
through the mourning,
through the night,
even if the sun and the earth collide,
j'ai créé un monde
it breathes,
it is alive.
this abnormally convoluted otherworldly world
that i created in my mind,
it is immortal; it will never die.

foolish

i'm so tired of me.
i'll set myself a timer,
call myself a writer,
fantasize of pouring gas all over me and kissing
the flame of a lighter,
engulfing myself in fire.
and you'd think it's dire,
but i'm just counting down the seconds 'til i'm
reduced to ashes.
i really need sleep.
when i stay awake through the night,
demons cling to me during the day.
even if i wish them away,
they say they'll never leave until i lay me down
to sleep.
i pray the lord my soul to keep.
suddenly, i'm made of screams.

reverie

sometimes i close my eyes to feel like i'm flying
feel like i'm falling
pretend that i'm dying.
i close my eyes
to fanatsize
and then fall asleep.
my eyes close and i start to float
to a world i want to see,
a girl i want to be.
where i'm entertained and never afraid.
my world will never be that way.
i am disenchanted, scarred, stained.
but i will escape.
if only for eight hours a day,
'til the black ink of night fades away,
the sky dissolves into grey,
and melts into day.
and i will sleep in an extra three hours
in denial that i'm alive to see another mourning.

bipolar II

existing in slow motion
i forget how to breathe
i have wept enough to flood the lakes, the ocean,
the sky, and the sea.
i'm trudging through the snow
sinking into a deathly winter's episode.
time moves slow.
i am engulfed in quicksand.
i can't move my body,
i can't move my hands.
burning in the flames
of dante's inferno.
this is a circle of hell
i didn't know existed.
suspending into darkness,
rising in the morning is the hardest.
i am unaware of anything outside of the cage
behind my eyes,
barreling toward defeat,
going down without a fight.
ears ringing and eyes blind in every sense of the
word.

i hyperfixate on the people i've hurt,
millions of hourglasses ago.

when i was trapped in the web of a manic
episode.
my mouth seemed to have a mind of its own.
talking to me was like walking on a landmine.
with bombs and blows,
i am bursting but i cannot seem to explode.

my voice breaks as i try to stabilize.
i've got a sick mind that was doomed from the
start,
with a bleeding wreck of a heart
that makes me do things i cannot begin to
understand.
my skin crawls as i realize i do not know who i
am.

where am i going?
there's no way of knowing.
spinning out of control and my eyes are glowing.

i am falling apart
faster than the tears bursting from my eyes like
the rapids.
razor blades are more patient
i feel the growing lacerations
stretching across my aching heart.
i'm sorry i'm not listening.
what's your name again?
i've met you before,

but i can't seem to remember.
your eyes reminded me of something a few
years back in december.
i know you wish i was different.
i think you want me to go.
so i will leave.
but on my way out,
i only want you to know
i'm going through something that you don't
understand.
and i don't expect you to.
but please just know
that i'm sorry.

king saul's torment

i don't know if i can explain it just right but i'll
try.

it's like a motionless ocean with no floor,
a windowless room with no door,
when the wine is poisoned and you feel dirty and
impure,
an alarm going off
no snooze button, no outlet, no plug,
you just have to wait for it to stop.
it's hard to describe
what happens when you fist-fight your own
mind.
it's bloody and cruel,
ugly, merciless, and makes you look like a fool.
it is like walking a fine little white line
and trying not to be swept away by the tide.
all i do is lie.
i will be fine.
it takes time for the clouds to disappear and the
sun to decide
it's safe to come out.
it shines on my ice-cold skin.
i try to warm up and feel better,
but then i get scared,

my vision is impaired,
i lose my balance and the tide sweeps me away
again.

eros

my entire being aches when i think of you.
and i can't help that at every moment of every
day,
all i want to do is be right next to you.
but all i feel is unrequited.
it's so real and so uninvited.
i only see what i want so badly to be:
you with me.

what if i went into the forest all alone?
would you come and find me?
i gazed over the edge of a bridge.
i stood there for days just trying to live,
to find a way to breathe without you with me.

i wrote poetry on my hands
and fell to my knees.
i cursed your name and let my tears dry with the
breeze.
the wind ripped gently through the trees,
sending leaves flying all around me.

i laid in the damp grass on the coldest, hardest
ground.
i painted a semi-permanent frown

on my face with the ink of my pen
that is the color of nightmares and sin.
i let the wind blow the wet ink around my red
cold burned up cheeks,
and the thought that i have real human skin is
only make believe.

but don't worry about me.
am i okay? hardly!

my hands are stained crimson from killing the
time with useless things
while my soul tells me to die.
by the angry blood stains and the ink on my
face,
you can tell that i'm in pain.
until it starts to rain,
and the tears drain.
the colors of fears and bad dreams fall away,
and now you can see the look on my face.
though the blood has rinsed from my hands,
the bleeding stains remain.

all this to say,
i miss you.

www.ingramcontent.com/pod-product-compliance
Lightning Source LLC
La Vergne TN
LVHW041246200726
843507LV00013B/2837